How to

SAIL A DINGHY

a step·by·step guide

Author:
Liz French

Technical consultant:
Geoff Evans,
Senior RYA instructor

JARROLD

Other titles in this series are:

TENNIS	**SWIMMING**
SQUASH	**GOLF**
BADMINTON	**WINDSURFING**
CROQUET	**SNOOKER**
BOWLS	**GET FIT FOR SPORT**
TABLE TENNIS	

How to SAIL A DINGHY
ISBN 0-7117-0505-4
First published in Great Britain, 1990
Text copyright © Liz French, 1990
This edition copyright © 1990 Jarrold Publishing
Illustrations by Malcolm Ryan

Designed and produced by
Parke Sutton Limited, Norwich
for Jarrold Publishing, Norwich

Contents

Introduction

Sailing is one of the most exhilarating and pleasurable of sports, enjoyed by enthusiasts of all ages the world over.

Once known as 'yachting', a diversion exclusively for the rich, sailing today is accessible to almost anyone, thanks largely to the wide range of smaller, cheaper sailing craft developed in recent decades. There is certainly no need to buy your own dinghy, though you may want to do so later. In fact, the best way to start is with a course of lessons at a recognised sailing school or club. Here you will be provided with all the equipment you need and a qualified instructor will take you through the basic techniques and manoeuvres. Contact the Royal Yachting Association for details at RYA House, Romsey Road, Eastleigh, Hants SO5 4YA.

This book is intended to be used alongside your early sailing experiences. Of course, nobody can learn to sail without spending time in a boat, practising the various techniques and manoeuvres. But when you step into a dinghy for the first time you will need to know what you are doing. So read through the book first, and make sure you understand the principles involved. You can then refer back to various points as you learn more from being on the water. The specialist language of sailing can be particularly daunting to beginners and you will find the glossary at the back of the book useful for explaining unfamiliar terms.

You will notice a strong emphasis on safety throughout the book. This is not intended to alarm you, but it is important to be aware of, and have respect for, possible dangers and how to avoid them. You should not even consider sailing unless you can swim a distance of at least 50 yards. It is obviously safer to sail on inland, non-tidal waters if possible; extra care is needed for coastal sailing. Make sure you are thoroughly informed about wind, weather and tides whenever you sail, and ALWAYS sail within the limits of your own experience and ability.

Joining a sailing club is a good step for newcomers to sailing. Most welcome beginners, and as well as providing safe, supervised areas to practise, they offer opportunities for picking up tips from more experienced sailors, for entering racing events and for making new friends who share your enthusiasm for the sport. You may also find experienced sailors willing to let you crew for them — one of the very best, and most enjoyable, ways of gaining experience.

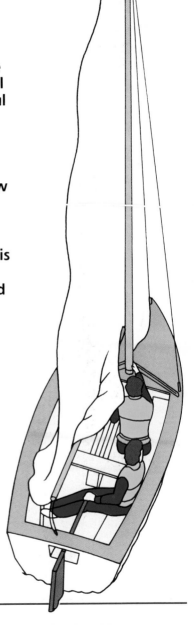

What is a Dinghy?

The different types of sailing boat can be a source of confusion to beginners. The term dinghy is used to describe any small, open sailing boat up to about 16ft long which has one mast and a retractable centreboard or a daggerboard instead of a fixed metal keel. A dinghy can be sailed or rowed and is light and easy to manoeuvre. Here several different types of dinghy are illustrated to show you some of the differences.

Single-hander

- around 6–7 ft long
- removeable daggerboard
- single sail
- suitable for children from about 6–15 years
- can be transported on car roof-rack

Example: Optimist

Small one- or two-person dinghy

- around 10ft long
- retractable centreboard
- mainsail and jib
- suitable for children and adults

Example: Mirror

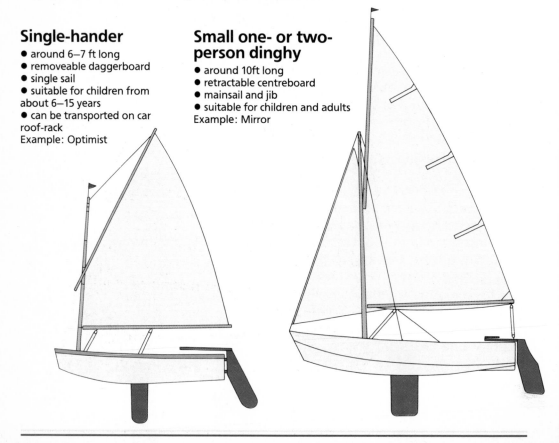

Larger two-person dinghy

- around 11–16 ft long
- retractable centreboard
- mainsail and jib
- suitable for adults

Example: Wayfarer

Clothing

Whilst there is no need to spend a lot of money on special clothing for sailing, it is essential you dress sensibly for warmth, dryness and freedom of movement. A good basic rule of thumb is to take one pullover more than you need on shore. Even if the weather feels warm, remember that the wind and spray will soon cool you down. It is far better to take too much clothing than too little – you can always remove a layer if you get hot. NOTE: A lifejacket or buoyancy aid is essential (see page 10).

Your body

Wear a warm pullover and trousers, topped off with any of the following:

Waterproof all-in-one   **Oilskin**   **Wetsuit**

● **Waterproof all-in-one**

Lightweight for freedom of movement.

● **Oilskins**

Worthwhile investment if you aspire to offshore cruising later, but rather cumbersome and will restrict your movements on a small craft.

● **Wetsuit**

Works by trapping a layer of water to act as insulation between the suit and your skin. Different types are available and can often be hired from clubs and training schools. If you buy one, make sure it fits snugly. A very lightweight wetsuit will need an overall over the top to prevent damage and chill.

Your head

About a third of body-heat loss is through the head, so wear a hat in cooler weather. Even if your all-in-one is hooded, a warm hat or balaclava will be needed on cold days. Don't wear a bobble hat, though — it could get caught up in the rigging.

Your hair

If you have long hair, wear it up or tied back — it could get caught in the rigging and will in any case be blown about making it harder for you to see where you are going.

Your feet

Obviously, shoes with heels are unsuitable. Any kind of soft-soled, non-slip shoes will do — plimsolls are fine. NEVER sail in bare feet.

Even if you don't capsize, you feet will get wet when launching and recovering the boat so some kind of waterproof over-shoe protection is sensible. Some people wear long neoprene socks under their sailing shoes. A cheap way of improvising is to wear woollen socks with plastic bags over the top, sealed with rubber bands. You can take these off once you get going. Sailing boots are available but are rather cumbersome for use on small craft.

If you are intending to buy any specialist clothing or equipment, it makes sense to check what is available first: look through magazine advertisements, browse round specialist shops and ask other users for advice.

Lifejackets and Buoyancy Aids

Even if you can swim well, it is ESSENTIAL to wear some kind of lifejacket or buoyancy aid.
If you are learning at an approved sailing school, you will certainly be provided with one.
Otherwise, go to a specialist chandler or good department store and buy one of your own.
To make sure that you buy a large enough size, it is a good idea to go shopping in the clothes
you would wear for sailing. But in any case, ask the assistant for advice on fit.

A properly made and fitted lifejacket would
provide enough buoyancy to support you in a
face-up float, even if you were knocked
unconscious. The most common type has some
built-in buoyancy but is only fully inflated in an
emergency, by mouth. However a full lifejacket
is too cumbersome for the small sailing craft
most people learn on, and you are more likely
to be given a buoyancy aid.

A buoyancy aid is a kind of padded waistcoat.
It should be easy to fasten and unfasten, with
a zip or buckle, and be lightweight and not
too bulky.

**Whether you are wearing a lifejacket or a
buoyancy aid, make sure it fits properly and
is correctly fastened — and look for British
Standard BS3595 and the BSI 'kitemark'.**

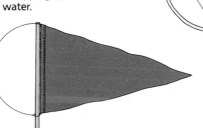

Other Equipment

Your dinghy should also carry some other equipment:

• One or preferably two paddles

In case you are becalmed or cannot sail back to shore for any other reason. Some craft may have oars instead.

• Sponge

For mopping up small amounts of water.

• Bucket or bailer

For removing large quantities of water from the boat.

• Sailing knife

Stainless steel type — handy for all kinds of jobs on the boat; keep it on a length of line tied to your waist.

• Pennant

A triangular pennant to fly at the top of your mast: this helps you judge the direction of the wind and lets others know you are cruising, not racing (a square flag indicates that you are racing).

• Hand-held orange smoke flare

Only really needed for offshore sailing.

• Anchor

A small anchor and line is very useful for coastal sailing but is not usually needed on inland waters.

Make sure that all your equipment is stowed safely and tied down, and that you know how to get to it.

A Typical Dinghy – The Hull

Here you can see inside a typical two-person dinghy. This is, of course, not the only kind of dinghy you could learn on, but although boats vary you will find most of the components are similar.

Painter – rope at the front (bow) of the boat for moorin or towing

Mainsail – see pages 14–15

Kicking strap – rope which prevents the boom from rising

Boom – wooden or metal spar into which the bottom of the mainsail is slotted

Fairleads – rings for guiding sheets to the right part of the boat

Thwart – seat running across the middle of the dinghy

Centreboard casing – houses the centreboard

Mainsheet – rope for adjusting mainsail via the boom

Buoyancy tank – compartment containing air to keep the boat afloat if it capsizes or becomes swamped

Cutaway view of centreboard in its casing showing three positions

Toestrap – for putting your feet under when leaning back (sitting out)

Transom – the flat end of the stern

Drainholes

Stern – the back of the boat

Universal joint connecting tiller and tiller extension

Rudder – changes direction of the boat

The Hull

Gooseneck — fitment for attaching boom to mast

Mast — supports the sails

Forestay — supports the mast from the front

Jib — see pages 14–15

Plates — for connecting the shrouds and forestay to the deck. Some boats have bottlescrews instead

Bow — front of the boat

Cleat — for securing rope, here the halyard

Shrouds (or sidestays) — two side wires which, together with the forestay, support the mast

Halyard — rope/wire for hoisting the sail

Mast step — takes the heel of the mast

Jamming cleat — for holding in the jibsheet

Jibsheet — rope for controlling the angle of the jib

Hull — body of the boat excluding mast and rigging

Centreboard — retractable fin which reduces the sideways slip (*leeway*) of the boat

Tiller extension

Tiller — for operating the rudder

The forestay (and shrouds) is attached to the hull with plates

The bottom block of the kicking-strap: once tightened the rope is jammed in the slot

A Typical Dinghy — The Sails and Rigging

Most dinghy sails are triangular. They are usually made of a tough synthetic material such as terylene that won't rot. Sails work by being set at precise angles to the wind. The ropes used to control the sails are together known as the running rigging and consist of halyards for hoisting the sails, sheets to control their angle and other lines such as the kicking strap for adjusting their shape.

Mainsail — larger sail set behind the mast

Battens — removable wooden or plastic strips to keep the sail's shape by supporting the leech

Groove in boom for bolt-rope to slide into (see pages 16–17)

Batten pockets — for housing the battens

NOTE: The smaller, one-person dinghies such as the Optimist and Topper are more simply rigged. These have only one sail which is sometimes sleeved onto the mast. The mast is then stepped into a hole in the deck and is left freestanding.

Leech — back, trailing edge of the sail

Clew — bottom back corner of the sail

Bolt-rope — sewn into the foot and luff; fits into grooves in the boom and mast

Foot — bottom edge of the

This diagram shows you the sails and their various parts for a typical two-person dinghy. They consist of the mainsail, set behind the mast, and the smaller jib, in front of it. You may also have heard of a spinnaker. This is an optional, balloon sail which can be fitted to some racing dinghies when sailing downwind but is not suitable for beginners.

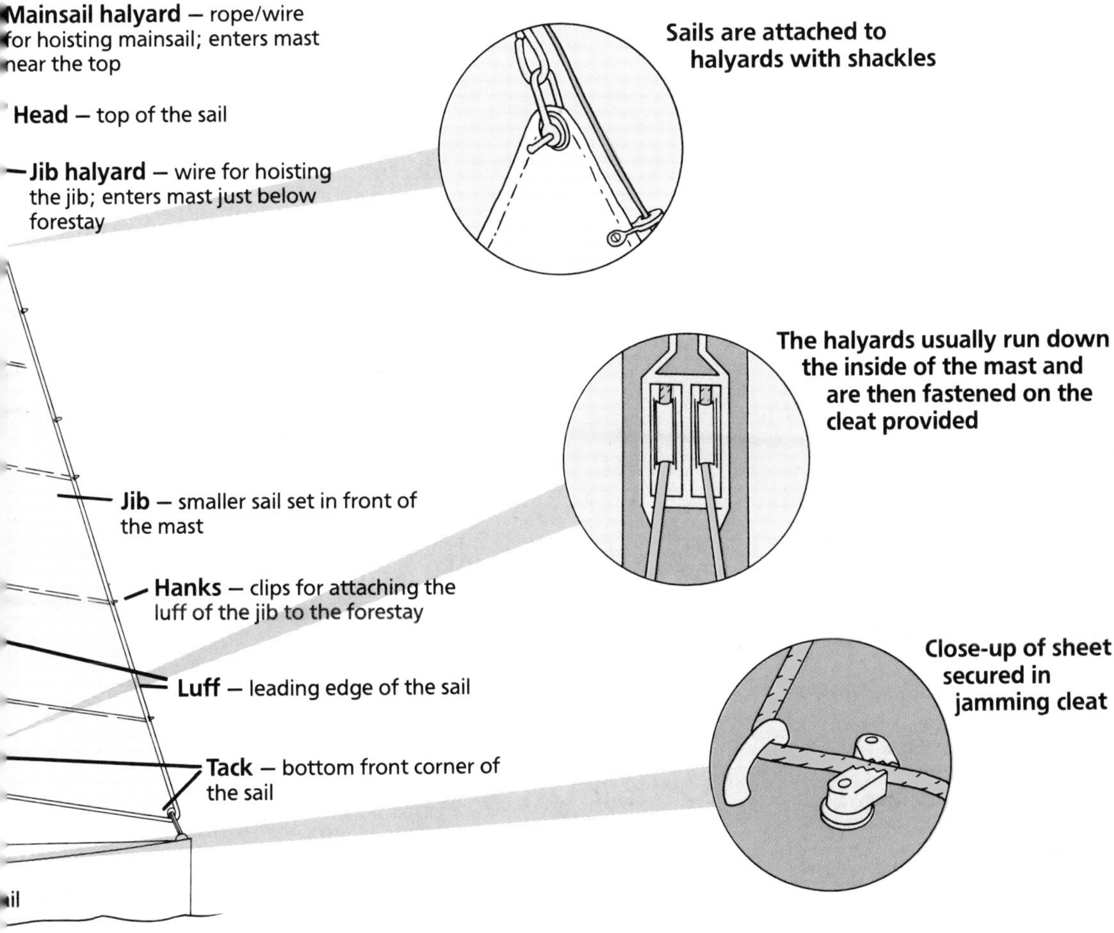

Mainsail halyard — rope/wire for hoisting mainsail; enters mast near the top

Head — top of the sail

Jib halyard — wire for hoisting the jib; enters mast just below forestay

Sails are attached to halyards with shackles

The halyards usually run down the inside of the mast and are then fastened on the cleat provided

Jib — smaller sail set in front of the mast

Hanks — clips for attaching the luff of the jib to the forestay

Luff — leading edge of the sail

Close-up of sheet secured in jamming cleat

Tack — bottom front corner of the sail

il

SAILING BASICS: BEFORE YOU START

Which Direction?

The wind is the source of power in sailing, and everything you do will be influenced by it. To get from A to B you will be sailing on a particular course. A course means the direction you are travelling relative to the position of the wind (and tide, if any) and the various courses are shown on the diagram below. They are usually known as the points of sailing. Whichever course you want to sail on, you will need to adjust the sails, centreboard and rudder for the direction of the wind.

No Go Zone

You will notice the shaded No Go Zone which extends for 45° on either side of the eye of the wind. It is impossible to sail on a direct course towards the wind – if you try to do so, the sails will just flap and the boat will slow down and stop. To sail upwind, you take a zig-zag course by tacking (see pages 32–33).

Port and starboard

Port and starboard basically mean left and right, from the point of view of someone facing forwards in the boat. PORT is the left side, looking towards the front of the boat; STARBOARD is the right. A boat is on starboard tack when the wind is coming over the right side of the boat and on port tack when the wind is coming over the left side.

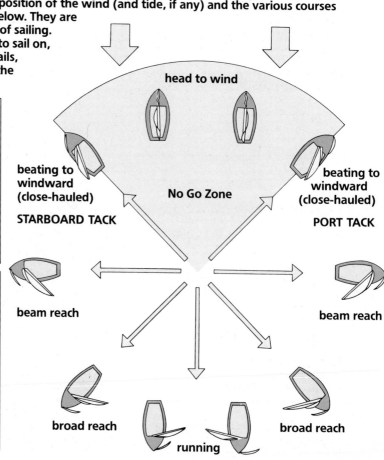

head to wind

beating to windward (close-hauled)

STARBOARD TACK

No Go Zone

beating to windward (close-hauled)

PORT TACK

beam reach

beam reach

broad reach

broad reach

running

Centreboard and Rudder Control

You already know that, for any sailing manoeuvre, you need to adjust the sails, rudder and centreboard. The various positions required for each course or change of direction will be explained in more detail on the following pages. But how do these controls work?

Centreboard

The centreboard (or daggerboard on some dinghies) helps reduce sideways movement (leeway). The faster you go, the more pronounced the effect. Centreboard position varies according to the point of sailing:

Sailing close to the wind
- maximum sideways force
- centreboard fully down

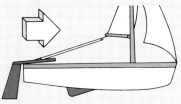

Sailing with the wind behind
- no sideways force
- centreboard almost raised ($\frac{1}{4}$ down)

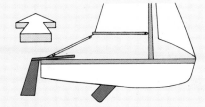

Sailing on a reach
- some sideways force
- centreboard in midway position ($\frac{1}{2}$ down)

Always raise the centreboard if the water is very shallow or it could stick in the mud!

Rudder

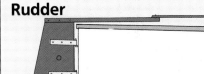

The rudder works by deflecting water as it passes the back of the boat, so obviously you have to be moving for it to have any effect. All you really need to remember here is that the boat will turn in the OPPOSITE direction to the way you move the tiller.

When the movement is completed, always return the tiller to the central position. Normally you hold the tiller extension in the hand nearer the stern, controlling the mainsheet in the other.

Fit the Mast and Sails

Before you can start sailing, you will probably have to fit the mast and sails. Some basic knots will be needed for this (see page 40). You should also check that you have all the items of equipment you will need and make sure you are aware of, and can handle, the weather and wind, and tides or currents if you are sailing offshore (see pages 22–23).

Fit the mast . . .

The method of fitting, or stepping, the mast varies from boat to boat. In simple single-handers like the Optimist the mast simply slots into a hole in the mast thwart. When stepping the mast, always check that there are no overhead power lines in the way.

1 For larger craft, two people are needed. First lay the mast on the ground, top of the mast pointing forward. Check that the forestay and shrouds are not tangled.

2 Raise the mast, then lift it into position.

3 Fasten the forestay and then one shroud, using the plates and clevis pins provided. Now, while one person holds the mast upright, the other can fasten the remaining shroud.

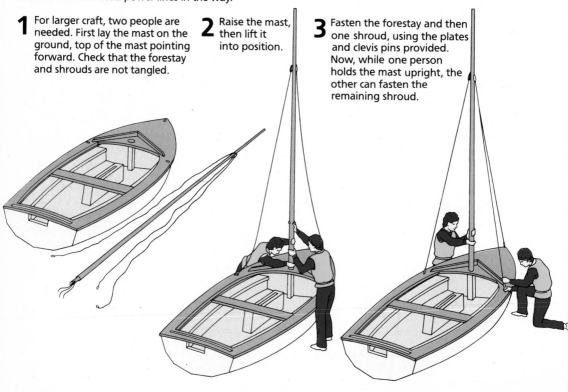

. . . then the mainsail . . .

1
Pull the mainsail from the clew through the groove in the boom.

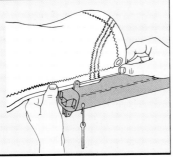

2
When the sail is fully inserted, fasten the tack with the pin provided.

3
Pull the sail taut and tie off; fix the mainsheet to the end of the boom.

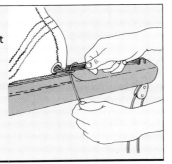

4
Fix the main halyard to the head of the sail with a shackle.

5
Insert the battens.

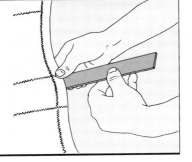

6
Feed a few inches of the bolt-rope into the bottom of the groove on the mast.

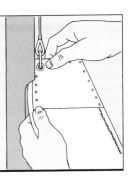

. . . now, the jib

1
Fasten the tack to the front of the boat with a shackle.

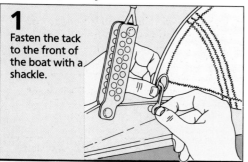

2
Clip the hanks onto the forestay.

3
Fasten the jib halyard to the head of the jib.

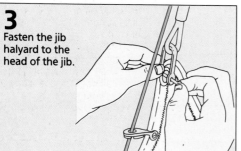

With the sails fitted but not yet hoisted, the boat looks like this. There is no need to fit the boom to the mast until you are ready to hoist the sails.

4
Fasten the jib sheets to the jib and lead them through the fairleads on either side of the boat. Tie a figure of eight knot (see page 38) 9in from the end of each jib sheet.

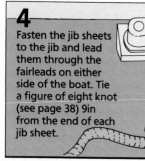

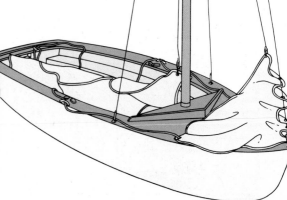

Reefing

Reefing is an accepted part of sailing even for very experienced sailors and is a means of reducing the size of the sail to suit the prevailing conditions and the competence of the helmsman and crew. As a beginner, you may need to reef before hoisting the sails even if the wind is fairly light. Reefing effectively gives you a smaller area of sail for the wind to catch: the method of achieving this varies according to the type of craft you are sailing. An Optimist requires no reefing at all; a Topper is very simply reefed by wrapping the sail around the mast until the area of sail is sufficiently reduced. Most other small dinghies are reefed by rolling the sail around the boom.

1 You may need to remove the lower batten if you are taking in a large reef.

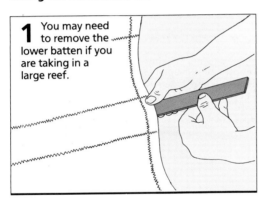

2 Unfasten the kicking-strap from the boom. Its attachment point will be covered by the rolled sail so you will need to fasten it another way. Most people roll a sailbag into the sail for this purpose. Put the boom on the gooseneck and hoist the sail as usual, tying the sail bag down to act as a kicking strap.

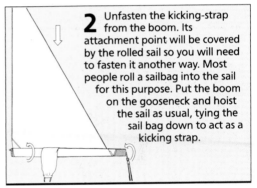

3 Take a tuck at the clew end of the sail. This will prevent the boom sagging.

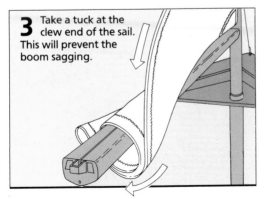

4 Now wind the sail around the boom by rotating the boom until the sail is reduced to the size required.

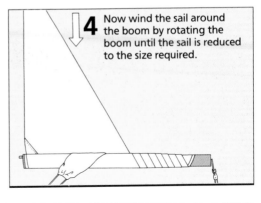

Safety Sense

Before you launch the boat, run through this safety checklist:

- How strong is the wind? Beginners should not sail if it is more than Force 3 (see page 46).

- Is the wind blowing away from the shore? Offshore winds are deceptive because the water can look calm. Beginners should NEVER sail in offshore winds.

- Is there a strong tide? If you can see water swirling around buoys and posts, there may be dangerous currents. Always heed warning notices and local advice. NEVER underestimate the strength of tides (see opposite).

- Get into the habit of checking weather reports in newspapers and on the television and radio.

- Check your equipment (see checklist opposite).

- Tell someone where you are going and when you will be back. Don't forget to tell them when you return.

- Are you near others? Always sail with a friend or with others nearby – it's more fun and safer.

If you have to signal for help:

- Slowly raise and lower your arms by your sides. This is the International Distress Signal.

- Stay with your boat: it will help keep you afloat and make you easier to spot.

- Above all, stay calm.

- Use flares if you have them.

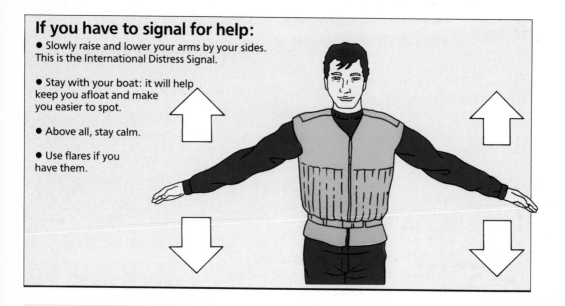

Equipment checklist

1 Is your clothing adequate (see pages 8–9)?

2 Is your lifejacket or buoyancy aid fitted properly?

3 Is your boat in good condition and properly rigged (see pages 18–20)?

4 Are all the hatches closed?

5 Are the drain holes in the hull closed and all bungs in place?

6 Is all your equipment safely stored and tied in?

7 If you are hiring equipment, it should be in good order, but do check for and report any signs of damage. Are there signs of wear on the ropes or mast fittings?

Tides

Tides are caused by the gravitational pull of the moon and sun and they change gradually from day to day. The tide takes about six hours to change from high to low, and its pull is strongest during the middle two hours.

The strongest tides – known as spring tides – occur just after the full and new moons. As a beginner, NEVER sail in an outgoing spring tide – if the wind dropped you could be swept out to sea.

Times and heights of tides are displayed in tide tables in newspapers, newsagents and chandlers in coastal towns.

Tide in or out?

If you can't find a tide table, look for these signs:

● WET sand on the beach means the tide is going out.

● DRY sand on the beach means the tide is coming in.

● Look at any boats that are anchored nearby. Unless the wind is very strong, they will have turned themselves to face the direction of the tide.

● Look at buoys and beacons: can you see bow waves or wake around them? These will indicate which way the stream is flowing past them.

● Are there any warning flags or signs about tides or currents? Always heed them.

Launching

Time to get the boat into the water . . .

1 First, you must find the direction of the wind — put up your pennant (use two clove hitches — see page 40) or hold up a hanky or a wet finger if you are not sure. Run the trolley down the slipway or ramp to the water and untie the boat.

2 Run the boat and the trolley into the water until the boat floats off, holding the painter. Recover the trolley and make secure — make sure you know what the tide is doing (see page 23) because you don't want it to be carried away by a rising tide!

3 Tie the boat up with the painter.

4 Climb aboard.

5 Point the bow of the boat in the direction the wind is coming from.

Leaving the Beach, Jetty or Mooring

The way you move off depends on where you are, and on the direction of the wind.

● If you are in a restricted space on a jetty, you will need to plan your route carefully to avoid other boats.

● If there is no tide, the boat will always point into the wind when moored. In tidal conditions, though, your boat may point into the tide, the wind or a combination of both. As soon as you untie the boat, it will start moving with the tide — so, again, plan your route to clear other boats.

● If there is a strong current or tide with a light wind blowing in a different direction, your boat may not be directly into wind. Your procedure will still be as above unless the wind is very light and the boat is turned completely away from the wind. Beginners would then be advised not to sail.

Under normal conditions, these guidelines will get you under way:

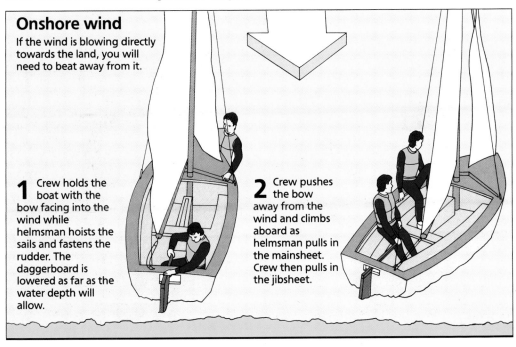

Onshore wind
If the wind is blowing directly towards the land, you will need to beat away from it.

1 Crew holds the boat with the bow facing into the wind while helmsman hoists the sails and fastens the rudder. The daggerboard is lowered as far as the water depth will allow.

2 Crew pushes the bow away from the wind and climbs aboard as helmsman pulls in the mainsheet. Crew then pulls in the jibsheet.

Hoisting the Sails

Now you are ready to hoist the sails . . .

1 Hoist the jib first, pulling on the forestay to get the sail up tightly.

2 Hoist the mainsail by inserting the luff of the mainsail into the mast groove and pulling it to the top with the halyard. Make off on the cleat provided.

3 Pull the boom down to the gooseneck with enough tension to just create a slight crease in the luff of the sail (adjust the gooseneck if necessary).

4 Tighten the kicking-strap and jam into the cleat.

5 Insert the rudder and tiller with its extension – remember to put in any retaining pins and fasten any control lines. Beware shallow water.

6 Insert the daggerboard if your boat has one, or move the centreboard into its halfway position (again, NOT if the water is very shallow).

Where should you sit?

Your position in the boat will vary a bit according to the course you are sailing and the strength of the wind, but if you can you should sit roughly halfway down the side so that you can easily manoeuvre the tiller extension. You (and your crew) should sit on the side opposite the sail – the windward side.

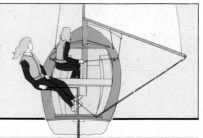

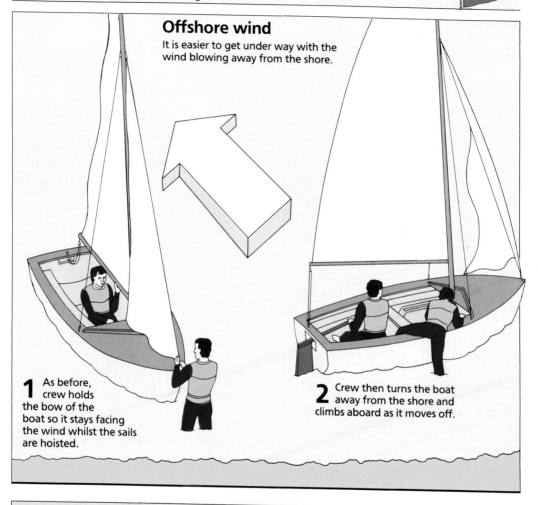

Offshore wind

It is easier to get under way with the wind blowing away from the shore.

1 As before, crew holds the bow of the boat so it stays facing the wind whilst the sails are hoisted.

2 Crew then turns the boat away from the shore and climbs aboard as it moves off.

For single-handers, the method is the same; you will need to get someone to hold the bow in position for you.

Returning to Land

When you are coming back to the beach, jetty or mooring, look and see how other boats are lying, to assess how your boat will end up. Plan your route very carefully, particularly if space is restricted. Your main problem is to slow down in good time to approach with full control. The boat has to be timed to stop just at the right moment for crew to grab the jetty or to jump out in shallow water.

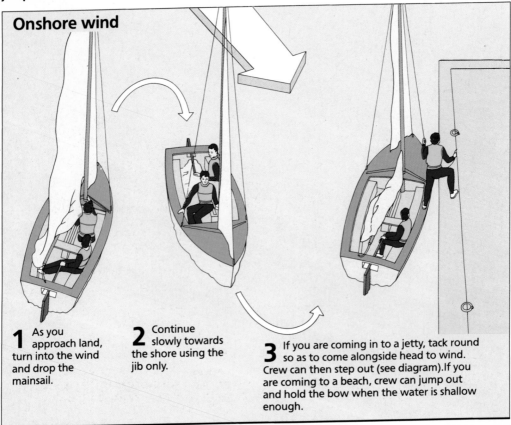

Onshore wind

1 As you approach land, turn into the wind and drop the mainsail.

2 Continue slowly towards the shore using the jib only.

3 If you are coming in to a jetty, tack round so as to come alongside head to wind. Crew can then step out (see diagram).If you are coming to a beach, crew can jump out and hold the bow when the water is shallow enough.

Offshore wind

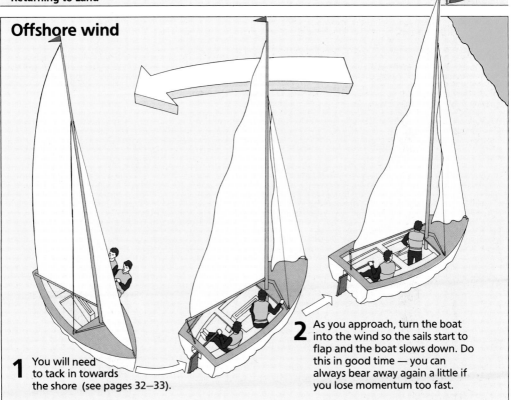

1 You will need to tack in towards the shore (see pages 32–33).

2 As you approach, turn the boat into the wind so the sails start to flap and the boat slows down. Do this in good time — you can always bear away again a little if you lose momentum too fast.

Remember:

● Raise your daggerboard in shallow water.

● If it all starts to go wrong and you find yourself on a collision course, turn around and approach again.

● If it's too late to turn around, remember that it is better to damage the boat than break your arm or leg. Trying to control a landing with your hands or feet when the boat is moving too fast is dangerous.

Basic Hove-to Position

When a sail is flapping it is producing no driving force. So if, at any time when you are sailing, you let out the sail until it flaps, the boat will stop and sit quietly in the water, almost at right angles to the wind. This is called lying hove-to and is a useful position to return to whenever you want to stop for any reason — for example, for a rest, or before starting a new manoeuvre.

You can return to the basic hove-to position from any course:

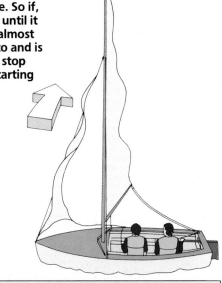

From a reach

Simply ease out the sail until it catches no wind and flaps. The boat stops. You may then let the tiller go (the rudder will only steer when the boat is moving).

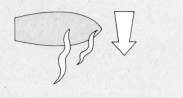

From a downwind course (broad reach or run)

First luff up to a reach, then ease out the sail as before.

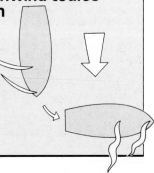

From a close-hauled course

First bear away to a reach, then ease out the sail as before.

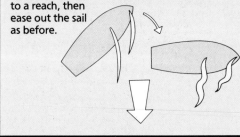

Note: To move forward again from the hove-to position, simply pull the sail in (sheet in) until it just fills with wind, and off you'll go.

Changing Course

Sooner or later you will want to turn the boat, either slightly away from the course you are sailing, or completely around. This is how to turn slightly closer to, or further from, the wind.

Luffing up

This means changing course to sail at a closer angle to the wind.

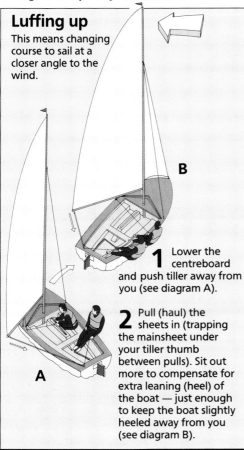

B

1 Lower the centreboard and push tiller away from you (see diagram A).

2 Pull (haul) the sheets in (trapping the mainsheet under your tiller thumb between pulls). Sit out more to compensate for extra leaning (heel) of the boat — just enough to keep the boat slightly heeled away from you (see diagram B).

A

Bearing away

Here you are steering onto a course further downwind — the opposite of luffing up.

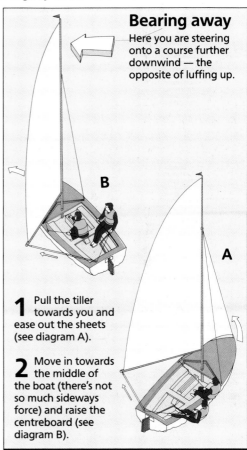

B

A

1 Pull the tiller towards you and ease out the sheets (see diagram A).

2 Move in towards the middle of the boat (there's not so much sideways force) and raise the centreboard (see diagram B).

Note: Remember to centralise the tiller when on the new course.

Tacking

If you want to sail towards a point directly upwind, you
will have to travel on a zig-zag course
crossing first on one edge of the No Go Zone
and then the other, turning the boat through
90° on each tack. Try to sail as close to the wind
as possible between tacks. The manoeuvre itself is
not hard to learn, but it does require co-ordination
because you are changing the sails – and your own position –
from one side of the boat to the other.

HELM	CREW
Bring the boat to close-hauled. Check that area is clear for the manoeuvre and call 'Ready about!' when you are about to tack.	Answer 'Ready'.
1 Pass the mainsheet to tiller hand and hold between thumb and tiller extension.	
2 Change tiller extension to free hand.	Jerk the jibsheet out of its cleat but keep it tight in your hand.
3 PUSH the tiller extension away from you. This will bring the boat towards the wind and the boom will swing to the middle of the boat. STAY WHERE YOU ARE until the boom crosses the centre line.	Let the sail be blown across and stay where you are.
4 Move forward with your front foot, duck under the boom, swivel to face stern and sit down on the new side. At the same time, rotate the tiller extension forward over the side of the boat.	Move across to the other side to balance the boat. Draw the sail in with the sheet and cleat it.
5 Bring the boat to close-hauled whilst trimming the mainsheet.	

Tacking in a two-person dinghy

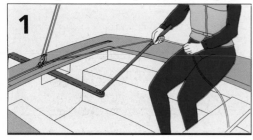

3

4

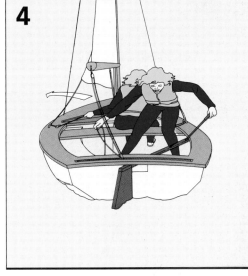

5

Single-hander tacking

1 Swap over the tiller and sheet from one hand to the other.

2 Push the tiller away and wait for boom to come across.

3 As the boat starts to turn, change sides, straighten the tiller and off you go on the new tack.

What do you do if you are stuck halfway through the tack with the sail flapping?

This often happens to beginners and is known as being in irons. Just push first the tiller away, then the boom. The boat will go slowly backwards. Pull in the mainsheet, then pull on the tiller to bear away. THINK: Push-push-pull-pull.

Gybing

A gybe is a way of turning when you are sailing with the wind behind you and is the opposite of a tack. So here, instead of turning into the wind, you turn further and further away from it until the wind crosses the stern of the boat. Remember that when tacking, there is a brief point of stability as the boat turns through the wind. When you are gybing, the wind is behind you throughout the manoeuvre. Hesitating could make you lose control and capsize, so once you have initiated the gybe, be positive and confident. Gybing is not easy to master, but remember, practice makes perfect.

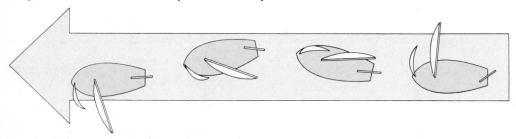

Gybing in a two-person dinghy

HELM	CREW
1 Start on a training run (see page 36), then pull in an armslength of mainsheet. Check that centreboard is only ¼ down, check that the way is clear for the manoeuvre and then say 'Stand by to gybe'. Change hands as you would for tacking.	Reply 'Yes'.
2 Reverse the tiller extension. Move to the middle of the boat facing aft and say 'Gybe Ho!' Push the tiller away from the side where the boom is.	Let go of the jib sheet.
3 Give a tug on the mainsheet. The boom starts to move across — duck to avoid it then sit out on the new windward side. Centralise the tiller.	Help the boom to move across by giving a tug on the kicking-strap. Move across with the boom and sit down to balance the boat.
4 As the boom finishes crossing, let the mainsheet back out.	Pick up the new jibsheet and sheet in the jib on the new side.

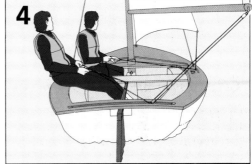

Hints for successful gybing

- The boat must be stable – not rolling – before you start the manoeuvre.

- Make sure the centreboard is in the correct position.

- Be ready to balance the boat.

- Be prepared to straighten course after the gybe.

- Above all, be positive!

Single-hander gybing

1 Swap over the tiller and sheet from one hand to the other.

2 Pull the tiller towards where you have been sitting and start to change sides.

3 Wait for the boom to swing across, then straighten the tiller and sit down on the new windward side. Remember to watch the boom and duck if necessary.

Training Run

You will at some point want to sail on a run, that is, with the wind behind you. Sailing on a dead run – with the wind directly behind – is not easy for beginners, because there is a risk of gybing inadvertently when the wind shifts slightly. To avoid this, try the following technique:

1 Bear away, letting out the main sheet until the boom is just off the shroud (NEVER sail downwind with the boom resting on the shroud – the leverage at the gooseneck can be very powerful).

bearing away

2 The jib will collapse and hang loosely.

dead run (goosewinged)

3 Just as the boat is heading directly downwind, it will flutter and try to fly goosewinged (that is, on the windward side, opposite the mainsail).

4 As this happens, immediately luff up slightly. This will bring the boat back to a position where the jib returns to the same side as the mainsail. You will now be sailing 10° off a dead run on a 'training run'.

10° off dead run

Trial Trip

Now that you have learned to sail in any direction, try taking a short triangular trip out from the mooring or beach and back again. Perhaps there is a buoy or marker you can head for; otherwise fix on a point, lining it up with a landmark to orientate yourself throughout the exercise.

Assume that the wind is blowing from the direction you want to go in, and the boat is hove to. Check the 'Points of sailing' diagram on page 16 to remind yourself what the different courses are called.

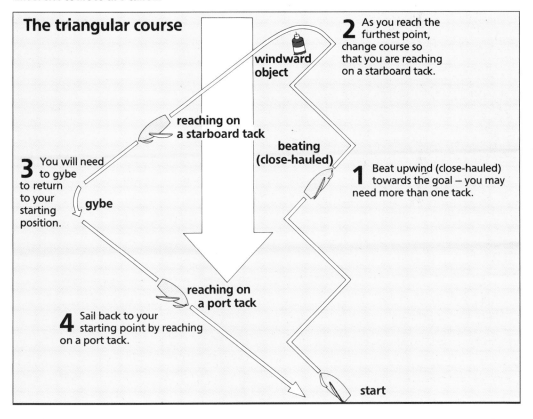

The triangular course

windward object

2 As you reach the furthest point, change course so that you are reaching on a starboard tack.

reaching on a starboard tack

beating (close-hauled)

3 You will need to gybe to return to your starting position.

gybe

1 Beat upwind (close-hauled) towards the goal – you may need more than one tack.

reaching on a port tack

4 Sail back to your starting point by reaching on a port tack.

start

How Efficiently Are You Sailing?

Each time you change course, check these points:

Balance

Are you keeping the boat on an even keel? It sails more efficiently if it is kept as flat as possible. If you let it heel to windward, it will tend to luff into the wind, losing you speed. If the sail is overpowered, and you can't control the heel by sitting out, let out the sheet a little.

Two-person dinghy

Helmsman sits on the windward side for maximum control and visibility so crew needs to adjust his position to keep the boat balanced:
● Light wind or downwind course: sit opposite helmsman.
● Strong wind: sit out on windward side when beating or reaching.

Single-hander

Always sit to windward and sit out as much as you need to to keep the boat on an even keel.

Trim

The fore and aft trim of the boat is also important.

Two-person dinghy

● Sailing windward: both move forward enough to raise the transom just out of the water.
● Sailing downwind: both move aft as wind increases to prevent bow nose-diving.

Sail Setting

For maximum efficiency, you must have the sails set at the right angle to the wind (see opposite).
● To find the most efficient point, let the sails out until the luff starts to flap, then sheet in until it just stops flapping. Recheck every time you change course.
● Remember: EASE OUT when you bear away; SHEET IN when you luff up (see page 31).

Centreboard

Always check the position of the centreboard when you change your point of sailing (see page 17).

Course made good

This means checking that you are taking the most efficient route to your goal. This is very rarely a straight line.
● Remember that even with the daggerboard fully down, on a reach or close-hauled course the wind will cause some sideways movement (leeway). You will need to take this into account when estimating your course.
● If you need to make some tacks, work out where to make them, and sail as close to the wind as you can in between tacks. Always tack in good time.

The Wind in the Sail

A little knowledge of how the wind acts on your sail will help you improve your sailing skills. It's certainly much easier to solve problems if you understand what is actually happening and why.

A sail works rather like the wing of an aeroplane, but whereas air flowing over an aircraft wing generates an upward force or lift, the force on a sail generates forward propulsion.

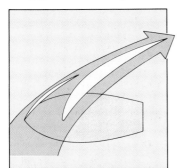

As the air meets the sail, it separates to pass either side. The curve of the sail makes the air accelerate leeward and this effect is increased by the jib. The different speeds result in an area of high pressure on the windward side, and low pressure on the leeward.

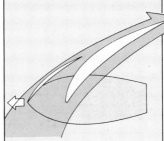

The sail is sucked into the low pressure area on the leeward side. The boat cannot move sideways very much because of the resistance of the centreboard. Instead, pressure builds up and the boat moves forwards.

If the sail is not angled correctly to the wind, the air flow breaks up and becomes turbulent and the boat will slow down.

Apparent wind

Apparent wind is the wind you actually feel when sailing. It is a combination of the true wind (what you'd feel if you were standing still) and the head wind created by the forward movement of the boat. The apparent wind will seem to come from further in front than the true wind, and the faster you go, the greater this effect. As you pick up speed, you will have to sheet in further to keep the sail at maximum power.

Knots and Hitches

These are some basic knots that you will need while sailing.

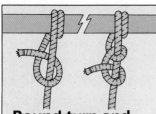

Round turn and two half-hitches

This is the simplest way of tying a line to an object. It is often used for mooring.

Clove hitch

Used in some boats to fasten the mainsheet to the boom, with a figure of eight knot added at the end (see below). It can more frequently be used with two half-hitches to make the boat fast, and for securing a pennant to its halyard.

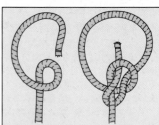

Bowline

This makes a useful loop at the end of a line and is another knot suitable for making the boat fast. On the Optimist it is used for fastening the kicking-strap to the boom.

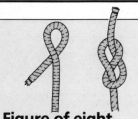

Figure of eight knot

Simple stopper knot used at the end of a sheet to stop it running out through a block or fairlead.

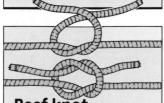

Reef knot

A knot with a variety of uses. On the Optimist a reef knot is used to secure the sail to the mast and boom. Easy to remember if you think: left over right — right over left.

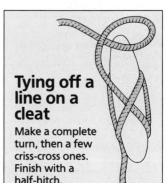

Tying off a line on a cleat

Make a complete turn, then a few criss-cross ones. Finish with a half-hitch.

Tie up the loose ends

Any spare rope or loose ends should always be neatly coiled up. If they are not, you might trip over them. They may also get tangled or knotted, making it difficult to get to the line when you need it again. A neatly coiled rope can often be hung up out of the way on a cleat.

SAFETY

Rules of the Road

Just as when driving on land there are rules for giving way to other traffic, so there are rules for avoiding accidents and collisions on the water which you must learn.

First, some general points of common sense:
- Try to show your intended course early.
- Always keep a good lookout.
- Try to anticipate.

These are important rules to remember:

Port tack gives way to starboard tack

If you are on a port tack, either bear away behind the other boat, or tack. If you are on a starboard tack, stay on the same course to allow other boats to keep clear. If the other boat doesn't seem to have seen you, hail them, and if a collision still looks likely, take avoiding action yourself.

Windward boat keeps clear of the leeward boat

If two boats have the same side facing the wind, the one which is sailing at the wider angle to the wind must keep clear. Again, if you have the right of way, steer a straight course to allow the other boat to change course and avoid you.

Overtaking boats keep clear of the slower vessel

If two boats are sailing the same course but one is coming up behind the other, it is the responsibility of the overtaking boat to keep clear of the one it is passing.

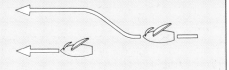

What about power-driven craft?

A sailing boat has right of way when meeting a power-driven boat of similar size. But this 'power gives way to sail' rule does not apply if you meet a large power-driven craft, or if you are in a river or estuary where the larger boat cannot move to avoid you without running aground.

Inland or Coast?

Whether you sail on a river or lake or on the sea will probably depend on where you live and what sort of sailing you want to do. Inland lakes and rivers are the safest places to learn, but you will eventually want to be more adventurous and try the extra challenge of coastal sailing.

Sea sailing

● The main difference between coastal and inland sailing is the influence of the tide. It cannot be over-emphasised that you MUST understand, and take account of, tidal conditions whenever you sail on the sea. See page 23 for how to identify tides.

● You should also check for other possible dangers such as rocks, shipping lanes or sandbanks. If there is a harbour bar, there is likely to be an area of rough water.

● Get local information — this is especially important when you are sailing in an area for the first time. The Harbourmaster, HM Coastguard, local fishermen and sailing club members will all be able to tell you of any hazards to look out for.

Lee shore problems

A lee shore is one with the wind blowing towards it — and if you are not careful you can find yourself blown onto it too! In rivers and estuaries especially this brings the possibility of running aground. If the bottom is muddy, you will feel the boat slow down and be unable to steer.

What to do

● Do not raise the centreboard initially — it is a natural reaction but will only make you drift closer to the shore.
● Until you are more experienced, the quickest way to get off a lee shore is to paddle or row away from it. In stronger winds you may need to lower the mainsail — make sure you are well away from the shore before hoisting it again.

Inland waters

Although there are less obvious dangers, there are some points to watch when sailing on inland waters.

● You may need permission to sail.

● Look out for local byelaws governing the use of the water. Are there any notices on the shore?

● Watch out for overhead power lines.

● If you are sailing on a river, there may be weirs or locks to negotiate.

Man Overboard

It's not too likely to happen, but you should know what to do if your helmsman or crew falls in. You will have to keep control of the boat on your own and return slowly and carefully to pick him up.

It is a good idea to practise this by throwing a buoy overboard and manoeuvering to come alongside it and stop in a hove-to position.

Remember:

● Keep the person in the water in sight all the time.

● Don't tack too soon.

● Approach slowly — concentrate on controlling your speed with careful trimming of the sails.

● He will be cold, wet and probably shocked, so make for home straight away.

2 When you are about 50-75 yds away, go about (tack) and return on a broad reach.

1 Whatever course you are sailing, come onto a beam reach and sail a safe distance away with the centreboard fully down. Keep the person in the water in sight.

3 Change towards a close-hauled course for the final approach.

4 Stop next to him by letting your sails flap, then move forward on the windward side.

5 Now the boat will be in a stable position, boom and mainsail out of the way, and you can help him back into the boat. Put your arm around a shroud so that you don't get pulled in too!

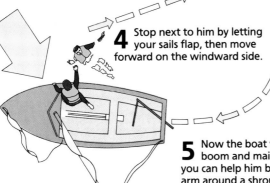

Capsize Procedure

Capsizing is the most common mishap in dinghy sailing. It is nothing to be afraid of: a good crew can be up and sailing again in less than a couple of minutes. Learning capsize procedure is an important part of any sailing course, and you will have to practise it!

Single-hander

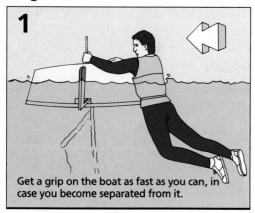

Get a grip on the boat as fast as you can, in case you become separated from it.

Pull on the centreboard or daggerboard with your hands and the boat will slowly start to turn upright.

If the boat has capsized into the wind, you may find that once it's righted it simply capsizes again but this time away from the wind. Try again! This time it should stay upright.

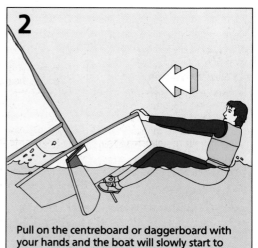

When the boat is righted, scramble aboard. Check your equipment and bail out any water.

Keeping Dry

Some single-handers (eg the Topper) are very easily righted. If you are quick enough during a capsize, you may be able to step straight onto the centreboard and right the boat immediately, avoiding a ducking.

Two-person dinghy

There are various ways of righting a dinghy with two crew people: this is perhaps the simplest. Again, the first rule is to stay with the boat. The second is to keep talking to each other — you won't always be in sight.

Both of you swim to the stern, and crew checks that the rudder is secure, then passes the end of the mainsheet to helmsman to use as a lifeline.

Both swim to the centre-board, helmsman going round the outside of the boat, crew inside. Crew checks that the centreboard is fully down and helmsman holds onto it (make sure helmsman is clear first).

Crew throws the top jibsheet over to helmsman, who calls out when he has it.

Crew stays in the hull, lying in the water but not holding on, as helmsman climbs onto the centreboard and pulls on the jibsheet.

The boat starts to right itself, 'scooping up' the crew member inside. Crew then helps helmsman in, near the shroud.

Bail out as much water as possible before sailing away. If you have self bailers, lower them when you are underway.

Note: If this procedure is unsuccessful, you must lower the mainsail and try again. If after several attempts you don't succeed you MUST stay with the boat and wait to be rescued.

The Beaufort Scale

Always check on the wind strength and direction before you sail.

Force	Description	Signs on the sea	Signs on land	Wind speed less than	Symbol
0	Calm	Mirror-smooth surface	Smoke rises vertically	1 knot	
1	Light air	Ripples but no foam crests	Smoke drifts with wind	1-3 knots	
2	Light breeze	Small wavelets with smooth crests	Wind felt on face	4-6 knots	
3	Gentle breeze	Large wavelets with crests starting to break	Leaves and small twigs moving; light flags will be extended	7-10 knots	
4	Moderate	Small waves becoming longer fairly frequent white horses	Dust and loose paper are lifted; small branches move	11-16 knots	
5	Fresh breeze	Moderate waves with frequent white horses	Small trees sway; waves on lakes inland	17-21 knots	
6	Strong breeze	Large waves start to form; spray likely	Large trees moving; whistling in telephone wires; difficult to use umbrellas	22-27 knots	
7	Near gale	Sea heaps up; and white foam from breaking waves blows with the wind	Whole trees bend; quite hard to walk against the wind	28-33 knots	
8	Gale	Moderately high, long waves; well-defined streaks of foam	Twigs break off trees; difficult to walk	34-40 knots	
9	Severe gale	High waves; dense foam streaks; crests roll over	Branches break off trees	41-42 knots	

Glossary

AFT — Towards the back (STERN) of the boat.

APPARENT WIND — The wind you feel as you sail along. A combination of TRUE WIND and HEAD WIND created by your forward movement.

BATTENS — Removeable plastic or wooden strips for stiffening the mainsail.

BEAM REACH — A course where the boat travels directly across the wind.

BEAR AWAY — To steer away from the wind.

BEAT — To sail UPWIND.

BLOCK — A pulley through which a rope is led.

BOLT-ROPE — Rope sewn into the FOOT and LUFF of the mainsail.

BOOM — Wooden or metal horizontal spar into which the bottom of the mainsail is slotted.

BOTTLE-SCREW — Device for attaching FORESTAY or SHROUD to the deck. Some dinghies have PLATES instead.

BOW — The front of the boat.

BROAD REACH — A diagonal downwind course.

CAST OFF — To untie the PAINTER when getting under way.

CENTRE-BOARD — Pivotable wooden fin which projects through the bottom of a dinghy to reduce LEEWAY. Some dinghies have a DAGGERBOARD instead.

CLEAT — Small device for securing a line.

CLEVIS PIN — Metal pin for attaching shrouds etc.

CLEW — Bottom back corner of a sail.

CLOSE-HAULED — A diagonal upwind course, as close to the wind as possible.

CLOSE REACH — A diagonal upwind course between a BROAD REACH and CLOSE-HAULED.

COURSE — The direction in which the boat is pointed.

CREW — The second person on a two-person dinghy; can also mean the whole team of a larger boat; see also HELMSMAN.

DAGGER-BOARD — Retractable wooden fin which projects through the bottom of a dinghy to reduce LEEWAY. Some dinghies have a CENTREBOARD instead.

DINGHY — Small open boat which can be sailed or rowed.

DOWNWIND — In the direction that the wind is blowing.

EASE OUT — See SHEET OUT; see also SHEET IN.

FAIRLEADS — Rings for guiding SHEETS or LINES to the right part of the boat.

FOOT — Bottom edge of a sail.

FORESTAY — Wire which supports the mast and is attached to the front of the boat; see also SHROUDS.

GOOSENECK — A metal fitting that secures the BOOM to the mast.

GOOSE-WINGED — When the jib is on the opposite side to the MAINSAIL when sailing downwind.

GO ABOUT — See TACK.

GYBE — To turn the back of the boat through the wind; see also TACK.

HALYARD — A rope used to hoist a sail.

HANKS — Clips for attaching the LUFF of the JIB to the FORESTAY.

HEAD — The top corner of a sail.

HEAD WIND — The wind created by the forward movement of the boat.

HEAVE-TO — To manoeuvre the boat into the basic HOVE-TO position.

HEEL — The leaning of a boat.

HOVE-TO — Position in which the boat is stationary with sails flapping.

HELMSMAN — The crew member who steers.

HULL — The body of the boat excluding mast and RIGGING.

JAMMING CLEAT — A CLEAT that instantly stops or releases a LINE.

IN IRONS — Position of a boat which is pointing directly into the wind, unable to steer in either direction.

JIB — Smaller triangular sail set forward of the MAINSAIL.

JIBSHEET — Rope for controlling the JIB.

Glossary

KEEL — Projecting fin on the underside of a yacht which reduces LEEWAY and acts as ballast. Dinghies have a DAGGERBOARD or CENTREBOARD instead.

KICKING STRAP — A tackle used for holding down the BOOM.

LEECH — The back edge of a sail.

LEEWARD — Anything downwind of a given object. The leeward side of the dinghy is the side away from the wind; see also WINDWARD.

LEEWAY — Sideways movement of the boat.

LINE — Rope.

LUFF — The leading edge of a sail.

LUFF UP — To turn the boat closer into the wind.

MAINSAIL — Triangular sail set just behind the mast.

MAST-STEP — Takes the bottom of the mast.

NEOPRENE — Stretchy, rubber fabric from which wetsuits and other protective clothing are made.

NO GO ZONE — Area of 45° on each side of the wind which can only be crossed by tacking.

OFFSHORE WIND — Wind blowing away from the shore.

ONSHORE WIND — Wind blowing onto the shore.

PAINTER — Rope attached to the front of a dinghy and used for MOORING the boat.

PLATE — Device for connecting FORESTAY or SIDESTAY to the deck. Some dinghies have BOTTLESCREW instead.

POINTS OF SAILING — Courses relative to the wind (see CLOSE-HAULED, BEAM REACH etc).

PORT — The left side of the boat looking forward; see also STARBOARD.

PORT TACK — When the boat sails with the wind coming over its right side.

REACH — See BEAM REACH, BROAD REACH, CLOSE REACH.

REEF — To reduce the size of the sail.

RIG — To prepare a boat for sailing by fitting the sails etc.

RIGGING — The wires and ropes used for controlling or supporting the sails, boom and mast.

RUDDER — Steering device.

RUN — A course with the wind directly behind.

RUNNING RIGGING — All the ropes and wires used for controlling the sails.

SHACKLE — Device for attaching sails, sheets etc.

SHEET — Rope for controlling a sail.

SHEET IN — To pull the sail towards you with the SHEET.

SHEET OUT — To let the sail out.

SHROUDS — Wires which support the mast and are attached to the side of the boat. Also known as SIDESTAYS.

SIDESTAYS — See SHROUDS.

SIT OUT — To lean back to balance the boat.

SPINNAKER — Balloon-like sail used on some dinghies when sailing downwind.

STARBOARD — The right side of the boat looking forward; see also PORT.

STARBOARD TACK — When the boat sails with the wind coming over its left side.

STEP — To erect the mast.

STERN — The back of the boat.

TACK — (1) To turn the nose of the dinghy through the wind; see also GYBE. (2) Bottom front corner of a sail.

THWART — Seat running across the dinghy.

TILLER — Handle which operates the RUDDER.

TOESTRAP — Strap on the floor of the dinghy, under which feet can be supported when SITTING OUT.

TRAINING RUN — A course 10° off a dead RUN.

TRANSOM — The flat end of the STERN.

TRIM THE SAIL — To adjust the position of the rig by SHEETING in or out to the optimum angle.

TRUE WIND — The wind you feel when standing still; see also APPARENT WIND.

UPWIND — The direction from which the wind is blowing.

WINDWARD — Anything upwind of a given object: the windward side of the dinghy is the side nearer to the wind; see also LEEWARD.

Printed in Italy.